N.M. BUTLER SCHOOL LIBRARY

Food For Good Health

GROWING FOOD WE EAT

Barbara J. Patten, MS

The Rourke Corporation, Inc.
Vero Beach, Florida 32964

© 1996 The Rourke Corporation, Inc.

All rights reserved. No part of this book may be reproduced or utilized in any form or by any means, electronic or mechanical including photocopying, recording or by any information storage and retrieval system without permission in writing from the publisher.

PHOTO CREDITS
All photos © Barbara and John Patten

Library of Congress Cataloging-in-Publication Data

Patten, Barbara J., 1951-
　　Growing food we eat / Barbara J. Patten.
　　p. cm. — (Food for good health)
　　Includes index.
　　Summary: Explains how we grow the food we eat, discussing such topics as soil, pesticides, and alternative forms of insect control.
　　ISBN 0-86593-401-0
　　1. Food crops—Juvenile literature. 2. Organic farming—Juvenile literature. 3. Agriculture—Juvenile literature. [1. Agriculture. 2. Organic farming.] I. Title. II. Series.
SB175.P37　1996
631—dc20　　　　　　　　　　　　　　　　　　　　　　95-25218
　　　　　　　　　　　　　　　　　　　　　　　　　　　　CIP
　　　　　　　　　　　　　　　　　　　　　　　　　　　　AC

Printed in the USA

TABLE OF CONTENTS

How Does Your Garden Grow? 5

Plants and How They Grow 6

Growing More Food 8

Too Much of a Good Thing? 11

DDT—A Scary Pesticide............................. 12

Safer Farming and Pest Control................ 14

Farm Soil 17

Using Natural Nutrients............................. 18

Insect Control 20

Glossary 23

Index 24

HOW DOES YOUR GARDEN GROW?

Crops, those plants grown on big farms and in backyard gardens, give us most of the food we eat. This makes how plants are grown important to us all.

Many farmers use **artificial** (art i FISH el), or made by people, **fertilizers** (FERT i liiz erz) to feed their crops, and control insects and weeds. Others use **organic** (or GAN ik), or natural, ways of growing food because they think it's safer and healthier.

Let's read all about these two different ways that farmers use to grow the foods we eat.

Most of the food we eat comes from plants, like this apple from an apple tree.

PLANTS AND HOW THEY GROW

Plants are special. They give us fruits, vegetables, berries and nuts. Wheat, oats, rice and corn are plants called **cereals** (SEER ee ulz). Sugar, mustard, licorice, and even peppermint, come from plants.

Most plants we eat start from seeds. Their main parts are the root, stem, leaf, flower and the fruit.

Corn plants will produce ears of corn.

Fresh ears of corn are a good source of vitamins.

The root and the stem grow from the seed. Roots hold the plant in the ground and take in water and **nutrients** (NOO tree ents) from the soil into the stem.

Water and nutrients are carried to the leaves that, like little kitchens, make them into foods the plants can use.

As the plant grows, the flower becomes the fruit—the part people eat. New seeds grow in the fruit.

GROWING MORE FOOD

Plants need sun and water. They also need soil rich in nutrients and protection from pests like insects and weeds.

Years ago, when the world started to fill up with more and more people, **botanists** (BAH tin ists), or plant scientists, wanted to get plants to produce more food without taking up more space.

After research and experiments, scientists invented artificial plant foods. **Pesticides** (PES ti siidz), pest control sprays and dust, were invented. They helped plants make more food and feed more people.

For sale: freshly picked vegetables are tasty and healthy.

TOO MUCH OF A GOOD THING?

Over time, many farmers came to depend on the chemicals—fertilizers and pesticides. Some no longer used organic ways to feed plants and control plant disease, weeds and insect pests.

After a while, people found out that when the new farm chemicals were not used safely, they were dangerous. They could **pollute** (puh LOOT), or poison, the farm soil, underground water supplies, and nearby ponds and rivers.

Misused farm chemicals can also harm the food we eat. Some pesticides cannot be washed off. People could be eating pesticides with their food.

Baskets of bright peaches are sweet-tasting and good for you.

DDT—A SCARY PESTICIDE

Artificial pesticides are used to control insects that gobble up tons of food grown for people each year. Scientists, however, worry that some pesticides are harmful to our health, air, water and soil.

One dangerous pesticide is DDT. For almost 30 years, DDT was sprayed on land and water to kill plant-eating insects and disease-carrying mosquitoes.

Years ago, dangerous pesticides got into rivers. Today, people are more careful.

12

Pelicans were harmed by the pesticide DDT.

Pelicans, eagles and other big birds started dying. Scientists found out that their eggs couldn't hatch because of DDT. Young birds weren't being born.

When people understood the danger they banned DDT. Over time, bird life has returned to normal.

SAFER FARMING AND PEST CONTROL

Today, we understand artificial fertilizers and pesticides better than we did in the early days of DDT. This has helped make our food safer.

Caring farmers use chemicals in smaller amounts and use pesticides in less harmful ways. Companies that make these chemicals try to find ways to make them safer.

Many people, however, think that organic farming is the safer way to grow and protect crops. Most organic farmers don't use chemicals.

A pesticide sign warns people to keep out of an apple orchard.

FARM SOIL

Farm soil is not just plain old dirt. It is a living system, made up of many parts that all work together.

Good growing soil is a mix of small rocks, air, water and organic matter like decaying or rotting plants.

Healthy soil has living things in it. Tiny soil bacteria help plants decay, and worms make tunnels that let water in.

Soil is made up of many different parts.
Plants use nutrients in the soil to live and grow.

USING NATURAL NUTRIENTS

All growing plants get nutrients from soil. Organic farmers add natural fertilizers to the soil to keep it rich.

Manure, body wastes from plant-eating animals like cows, is the natural fertilizer farmers use most. Plowed into the soil, manure puts back many nutrients used up by the last plant crop.

Cow manure is a natural fertilizer for soil and plants.

Watermelons wait to go on a picnic. They are a healthy snack.

Compost (KAHM pohst) also puts back soil nutrients. Compost is natural plant food made from decaying or rotting grass and leaves, skins and stems from fruits and vegetables, and coffee grinds.

Compost is all natural and doesn't pollute. It feeds the soil that feeds the plants.

INSECT CONTROL

Organic farmers use natural pest controls like garlic oil, hot pepper spray, tobacco dust, plant oils and plain soap. They stop insect pests, don't harm the soil, and easily wash off fruits and vegetables.

Some animals work great at pest control, too. Fruit growers can use non-poisonous snakes to eat tree rodents that hurt trees.

One toad in a garden eats between 10,000 and 20,000 insects in a growing season. In some places, farmers keep flocks of ducks in the fields to eat insect pests.

Some farmers use ducks to control insects.

GLOSSARY

artificial (art i FISH el) — made by people

botanists (BAH tin ists) — plant scientists

cereal (SEER ee ul) — wheat, oats, barley, rye, corn

compost (KAHM pohst) — natural plant food

fertilizer (FERT i liiz er) — plant food

nutrients (NOO tree ents) — chemicals in food that plants and people use to live and grow

organic (or GAN ik) — natural

pesticides (PES ti siidz) — artificial pest control sprays and dusts

pollute (puh LOOT) — poison

Organic foods are available in grocery stores.

INDEX

artificial   5, 8, 12, 14
birds   13
botanists   8
cereals   6
chemicals   11, 14
compost   19
crops   5, 14
DDT   12, 13, 14
ducks   20
eagles   13
farmers   5, 11, 14, 20
fertilizers   5, 8, 11, 14, 18
insects   8, 11, 12, 20
manure   18
natural   5, 19, 20

nutrients   7, 8, 18
organic   5, 11, 14, 20
pelicans   13
plants   5, 6, 7, 8, 18, 19

631   Patten, Barbara J.,
PAT   Growing food we
        eat

DATE DUE

631   Patten, Barbara J.,
PAT   Growing food we
        eat

N.M. BUTLER SCHOOL LIBRARY

N.M. BUTLER SCHOOL LIBRARY